MORE THAN a REPORT

Nine Science Writing Projects

More Than a Report is a **unique** way to insure **successful, individual** report writing.

Unique - The polished look of the finished product, complete with a three-dimensional visual, makes these projects "more than a report."

Successful - The simple, structured format allows each student to complete reports regardless of skill level.

Individual - Students work on their own topics within the same theme. Students can work cooperatively while producing their own report.

More Than a Report appeals to all learning styles.

MORE THAN a REPORT

Materials List

Here are the materials you will need for the reports in this book. Materials for each report are also listed on the **Teacher Direction Page** for every report.

Most of the materials are everyday school supplies; a few will need to be purchased.

Needed for all reports:
- file folder or 12" x 18" (30.5 x 46 cm) construction paper folder per student
- copy paper - at least four pages per student for each report
- glue to attach reproducibles to the inside of the folder. Rubber cement gives the nicest results. However, this glue is **not** to be used by students. An adult will need to assemble the completed folders if rubber cement is used.
- markers, crayons, or colored pencils

Needed for some reports:
- odds and ends for the **Inventor's Bag** (see page 10 for details)
- colored construction paper
- cut file folders (see page 4 for details)
- corrugated cardboard (cut as directed)
- dirt and small leaves
- white glue
- glue gun (optional, but very helpful)
- foil stars
- clear plastic cups
- cotton
- bean seeds

How to Make **More Than a Report** a Snap!

Research Skills

The ability and experience level of your class will determine how much teaching or reviewing of research skills is needed. Obviously, these reports will be more successful if your class has had practice with research strategies, note-taking skills, and bibliography entries.

How to Assign the Reports

All reports will be individualized. An annotated list is provided following the teacher directions in each chapter. You can assign the report in several ways:

- let students choose their topic
- students pick a topic out of a hat
- you assign each topic
- assign reports alphabetically

Student Direction Sheets

All reports come with two "Student Direction Sheets." These will help you explain the report and guide your students along the way. Discuss every step of the directions with your students, modeling where appropriate. Assess understanding of each section before going on. Explain that the box in front of each step is for them to check off each completed step. The first time you do a report, keep samples or take pictures of finished products to use with future classes.

Hint: Make overlays of the reproducible forms for each report. Display them on the screen as you go over the directions, pointing out each section as it is explained.

Lined-paper Masters

The final copy of most of the reports is completed on unlined paper. To help students write neatly and in a straight line, make up a class set of lined masters:

- Take one sheet of ruled paper (the kind they use everyday).
- Trace over each line using a ruler and a fine-tipped black marker.
- Photocopy a class set.
- Laminate.

Students paper clip blank paper to the master; the guidelines show through.

Bibliography Formats

A number of **More Than a Report** projects require students to list resources used in a bibliography.

On the inside back cover, you will find a chart showing how to write bibliographic entries for several types of resources. Reproduce this chart for each student or post for student reference.

Three-Dimensional Visuals

Stand-Up Visuals

These visuals appear in the following reports: **National Parks** and **Desert Dwellers**.

Old (or new) file folders are a great source of stiff paper. Follow these steps to create file folder stand-ups.

1. Cut the file folder in half.

2. Trim the 9" width to 7" (double thickness).

3. Fold under 1" on both sides.

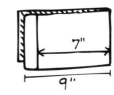

4. Draw a large picture.

5. Cut it out leaving a border around the image.
   The top remains connected at the fold.

6. Glue down the front folded lip.
   The whole picture can be laid down for storing.

7. Back extends to support the drawing.

Pop-Up Visuals

These visuals appear in the following reports: *Life in the Ocean*, *Save the Earth*, and *Endangered Animals*. A pop-up may have one or more pop-up tabs.

Provide each student with: a pop-up pattern (see pages 61, 70, 79), a piece of construction paper, paper scraps, scissors, glue, and felt pens or crayons.

1. With the printed side facing out, fold the page in half along the line.

2. Cut through both layers of the paper along the solid lines.

3. Open the page. Refold the paper so that the printed side is inside.

4. Gently pull the cut tab into the center, reversing the folds. Carefully close the pop-up on itself and press firmly to establish new fold lines.

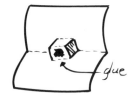

5. Open the pop-up and apply glue to the front of the pop-up tab. Affix the pop-up art.

6. Create a folder for the pop-up from an 8 1/2" x 11" (21.5 x 28 cm) piece of construction paper.

7. Lay the folded pop-up in the folder. Apply glue to the back of the pop-up page and press the folder closed.

8. Flip the folder over. Open the cover and apply glue to the back of the other side of the pop-up page. Close the folder and press firmly.

Inventions

An invention is something new and useful that someone has created. It may be a device or a process, simple or complicated, but unique in that it has never been done before. Anyone can be an inventor. You don't need to be a certain age or hold a certain degree. All you need is a new idea.

Students love to be creative. In this **More Than a Report,** students are given the opportunity to be creative inventors. You will prepare an inventor's bag for them to use in creating an **extraordinary** flying machine. It is a simple concept and easy to prepare, but the results will be as varied and unique as your students. This is a fool-proof, no-fail project. When they are finished, you have everything you need to put on an *Invention Convention*!

Get those creative juices flowing. This report can be a springboard for writing a science fiction story or inventing another type of machine.

Complete teacher directions for ***Inventions*** are on page 12.

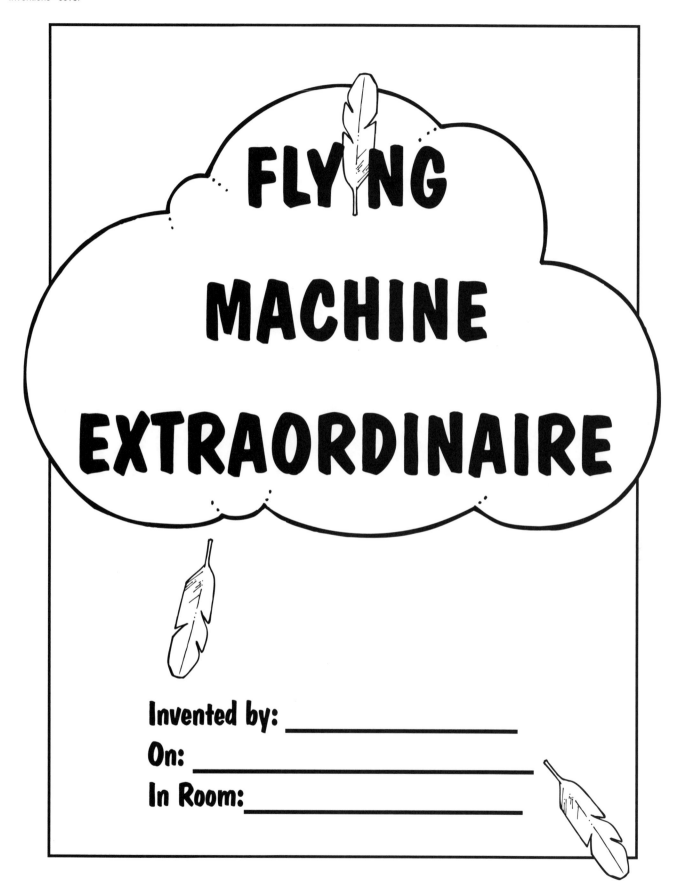

FLYING MACHINE EXTRAORDINAIRE

Invented by: _____
On: _____
In Room: _____

Flying Machine Extraordinaire

Invented by _____

Machine's name: _____

Top speed: _____   Maximum altitude: _____

Weight: _____   Height: _____

Type of fuel used: _____   Fuel capacity: _____

Fuel burned in one hour: _____

Maximum number of passengers: _____

Crew Members (full name, title, and job description)

1. _____

2. _____

3. _____

4. _____

5. _____

Special Features

Number of flight days: _____

Distance it can travel: _____

Constructed from: _____

Special features found inside for convenience of passengers:

_____

_____

_____

Name:_____

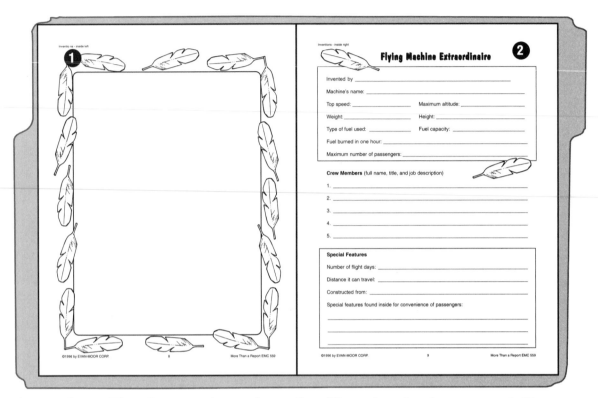

Instructions—The diagram above shows the different parts of your report. The numbers in your directions match the numbers above. This shows you where information is to be placed on your report. Keep these sheets in your folder so you can look at them often. You're going to do an ***extraordinary*** job!

☐ **Front Cover**
Your front cover is not pictured here. Complete the lines at the bottom. You may decorate the page any way you wish.

☐ ❶ **Your Flying Machine**
- Use the **Inventor's Bag** given to you by your teacher. Invent a flying machine by following the directions on the note stapled to the bag. Be sure to follow all the rules on the paper. When finished, your machine will be displayed in this space.

- Decorate this space to show what would be below your machine as it is flying (outer space, jungle, ocean, city, country, etc.).

- Decorate the *entire* space.

- Use lots of color.

Name:_____

☐ ❷ Information About Your Flying Machine

- Write your full name on the top line.

- Give your machine a unique name on the second line.

- Top speed should be labeled in kilometers per hour.

- Maximum altitude should be labeled in meters or kilometers.

- Weight should be labeled in kilograms.

- Height should be labeled in meters.

- Your machine can be fueled by any means you choose (gas, oxygen, jello, soda, peanuts, etc.).

- Fuel capacity should be labeled in liters.

- Fuel burned in one hour should be labeled liters per hour.

- Your machine can have more than 5 crew members, but you only need to give information for 5.

- Special feature information is from your own imagination. Use it!

Hints for completing a truly "extraordinary" report:

Be neat. Use your best handwriting.

Plan ahead when constructing your flying machine.

Think about what will make your machine unique.

Use your imagination and creativity.

Use lots of color.

YOUR REPORT IS DUE: _____

Before assigning the report:

Prepare the materials needed for each student:

- 1 file folder or folded 12" x 18" (30.5 x 46 cm) piece of construction paper

- a completed **Inventor's Bag** (see instructions, page 13)

- report reproducibles, pages 7, 8, and 9

- student direction sheets, pages 10 and 11 (fill in date due before copying)

Assigning the report:

1. Pass out to students:
   - folder and report reproducibles

   - an **Inventor's Bag**

2. Introduce the report.
   - Explain that each student will create their own **flying machine** from the entire contents of the **Inventor's Bag** (plus bag and note). Be sure to answer all questions at this time. Go over the rules on the note.

   - Students should follow along on their direction sheets as you explain each section of the report.

Working on the report:

Allow time in class to construct the **flying machines,** or assign the project as homework. Creating the flying machines at home adds an element of surprise.

Finishing the report:

- Glue the completed report cover to the outside of the folder.

- Glue the completed pages to the inside of the folder, one on each side.

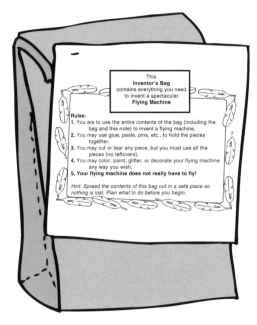

An Inventor's Bag

Instructions for putting it together:

You'll need one identically-sized paper bag per student. Colored bags add to the finished product. Sometimes fast-food restaurants give paper bags to teachers, so ask around.

Open up the paper bags and stand them next to each other. Now comes the fun part! You can put into the bags any items you wish, but YOU MUST PUT THE SAME ITEMS IN EACH BAG SO THEY ARE IDENTICAL. It is important that each student receive the same supplies. This makes the project much more entertaining. Some items you can include:

- paper clips
- length of string
- straws
- scrap paper
- paper cup
- rubber bands
- Popsicle® sticks
- Styrofoam® chips
- index cards

or anything you have in your supply closet or recycle box

When the bags are full, fold the top closed and staple on the note below.

This
Inventor's Bag
contains everything you need
to invent a spectacular
Flying Machine

Rules:
1. You are to use the entire contents of the bag (including the bag and this note) to invent a flying machine.
2. You may use glue, paste, pins, etc., to hold the pieces together.
3. You may cut or tear any piece, but you must use all the pieces (no leftovers).
4. You may color, paint, glitter, or decorate your flying machine any way you wish.
5. **Your flying machine does not really have to fly!**

Hint: Spread the contents of this bag out in a safe place so nothing is lost. Plan what to do before you begin.

National Parks

Congress laid the foundation of the U.S. National Park System in 1872 by establishing Yellowstone National Park. Today, the National Park System comprises more than 300 areas totaling 79,017,972 acres. National parks have been the continuing battlegrounds of the conservation movement. Originally, only specific things within a park were protected— wildlife here, geysers there. Today, environmentalists seek to save the entire **glorious** habitat. This means that people must not pick the flowers or collect rocks or shells. It also means a revolution in the way we appreciate nature.

In this **More Than a Report,** each student will have a chance to study one specific park. As students become aware of the beauty and wonder our National Parks offer, they will hopefully acquire a commitment to the maintenance of our fragile ecosystems.

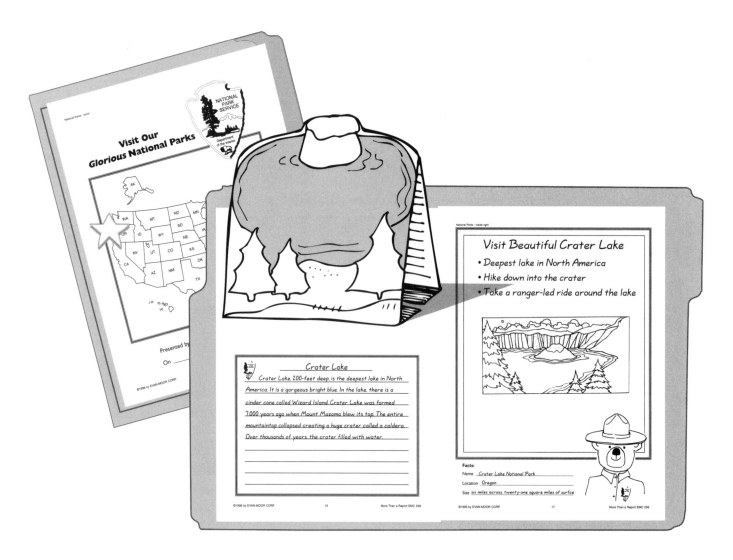

Complete teacher directions for **National Parks** are on page 20.

Visit Our
Glorious National Parks

NATIONAL PARK SERVICE

Department of the Interior

Presented by _____

On _____ From Room_____Teacher _____

glue here

NATIONAL
PARK
SERVICE

Department
of the Interior

_____

_____

_____

_____

_____

_____

_____

_____

_____

_____

Facts:

Name _____

Location _____

Size _____

Name: _____

The **national park** you are reporting on: _____

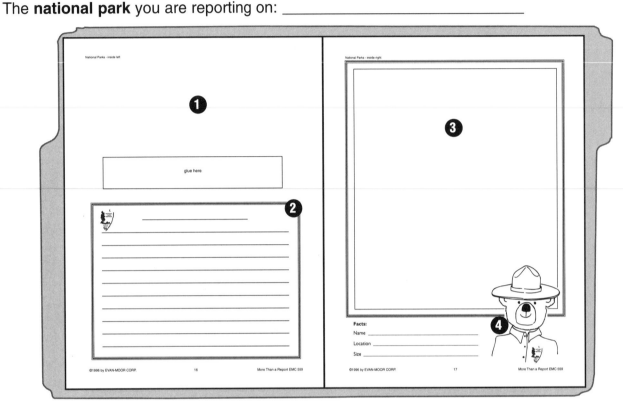

Instructions—The diagram above shows the different parts of your report. The numbers in your directions match the numbers above. This shows you where information is to be placed on your report. Keep these sheets in your folder so you can look at them often. You're going to do a *glorious* job!

Front Cover
Your front cover is not pictured here. To complete the front cover, follow these directions:
- Fill in the line with the name of your national park.
- Locate your national park on the U.S. map with a foil star. Color the map.
- Fill in the information on the lines at the bottom.

❶ Stand-Up Picture
Draw a picture of an important feature of your national park on the piece of file folder your teacher has given you.
- Keep the fold at the top.
- Make the picture large, touching the top and bottom. Color it.
- Cut out the picture. Cut through both layers. Leave a border.
- Glue the front lip inside the box. Do not glue the back lip.

Name:_____

☐ ❷ **Describe Your Stand-Up Picture**
In this space, describe the feature you have drawn.

- Write its name on the top line.

- Include as many facts as you can.

- Use colorful, descriptive language.

☐ ❸ **Create a Travel Poster**
It is your job to design a travel poster that will make people want to visit your national park.

- Include important points of interest.

- Draw a picture to go with your words.

- Make people want to read your poster.

☐ ❹ **Fill in the Facts**
- Be accurate.

- Write neatly.

Hints for completing a "glorious" report:

Be neat. Use your best handwriting.

Plan ahead before you begin.

Use lots of color.

Use your imagination and creativity.

NATIONAL PARK SERVICE

Department of the Interior

YOUR REPORT IS DUE: _____

Before assigning the report:

1. Your students will need to be able to do simple research and note-taking before attempting this report. If you feel they lack sufficient experience, pick a park from the list on page 21. Do the research and note taking as a group, with you modeling correct strategies.

2. Prepare the materials needed for each student:

   - 1 file folder or folded 12" x 18" (30.5 x 46 cm) piece of construction paper
   - report reproducibles, pages 15, 16, and 17
   - student direction sheets, pages 18 and 19 (fill in date due before copying)
   - cut file folder (see page 4)
   - foil star
   - index cards or note-taking paper

3. Decide how to assign each national park (see directions, page 3, and the list of parks on page 21).

Assigning the report:

1. Pass out to each student:

   - folder and report reproducibles
   - cut file folders and cardboard
   - student direction sheets
   - index cards or note-taking paper

2. Introduce the topic. Explain that every student will report on a different National Park. They should follow along on their direction sheets as you explain each section of the report.

3. Demonstrate how their stand-up picture will look after it is cut out.

Working on the report:

- Provide students with a variety of resources.

- Ask your librarian for support and classroom reference materials.

Finishing the report:

- Help students proofread work before it is transferred to the final copies.

- Glue the completed report cover to the outside of the folder.

- Glue the completed reproducibles to the inside of the folder; one on each side.

National Parks

The East

Acadia	Biscayne	Virgin Islands
Everglades	Voyageurs	Great Smoky Mountains
Hot Springs	Isle Royale	Mammoth Cave
Shenandoah		

The Southwest

Big Bend	Carlsbad	Guadalupe

The Colorado Plateau

Arches	Bryce Canyon	Canyonlands
Capitol Reef	Grand Canyon	Great Basin
Mesa Verde	Petrified Forest	Zion

The Pacific Southwest

American Samoa	Channel Islands	Sequoia & Kings Canyon
Hawaiian Volcanoes	Haleakala	Yosemite

The Rocky Mountains

Badlands	Grand Teton	Rocky Mountain
Theodore Roosevelt	Waterton-Glacier	Wind Cave
Yellowstone		

The Pacific Northwest

Crater Lake	Lassen Volcanic	Mount Rainier
North Cascades	Olympic	Redwood

Alaska

Denali	Gates of the Arctic	Glacier Bay
Katmai	Kenai Fjords	Kobuk Valley
Lake Clark	Wrangell-St. Elias	

More Than a Report EMC 559

Seeds

Any study of plant life should begin with the study of seeds. The fascinating observation that a *life-giving* seed contains everything necessary to reproduce its parent plant continues to amaze students of all ages.

In this **More Than a Report,** students will observe and record their observations about two different seeds sprouting.

One will be a quick growing bean seed that you will provide. The other one will be a seed they have brought from home. They should be able to identify the seed coat, the sprouting embryo, and the food the rest of the seed provides.

Enjoy this life-giving seed report. Let students have time for discussion and lengthy observation. Then let them decide what to do with the seeds after they have sprouted.

Complete teacher directions for **Seeds** are on page 28.

The Life-Giving Seed

Observations made by: _____

Teacher: _____ **Room:** _____

Beginning Date: _____

Ending Date: _____

Type 1 seed _____

Observations

Day 1 _____
_____
_____

Day 2 _____
_____
_____

Day 3 _____
_____
_____

Day 4 _____
_____
_____

Day 5 _____
_____
_____

Type 2 seed _____

Observations

Day 1 _____
_____
_____

Day 2 _____
_____
_____

Day 3 _____
_____
_____

Day 4 _____
_____
_____

Day 5 _____
_____
_____

More Than a Report EMC 559

Student Directions: Seeds - *A Life-Giving Report*

Name: ____

Life-Giving Seed **Type 1** ______________________________

Life-Giving Seed **Type 2** ______________________________

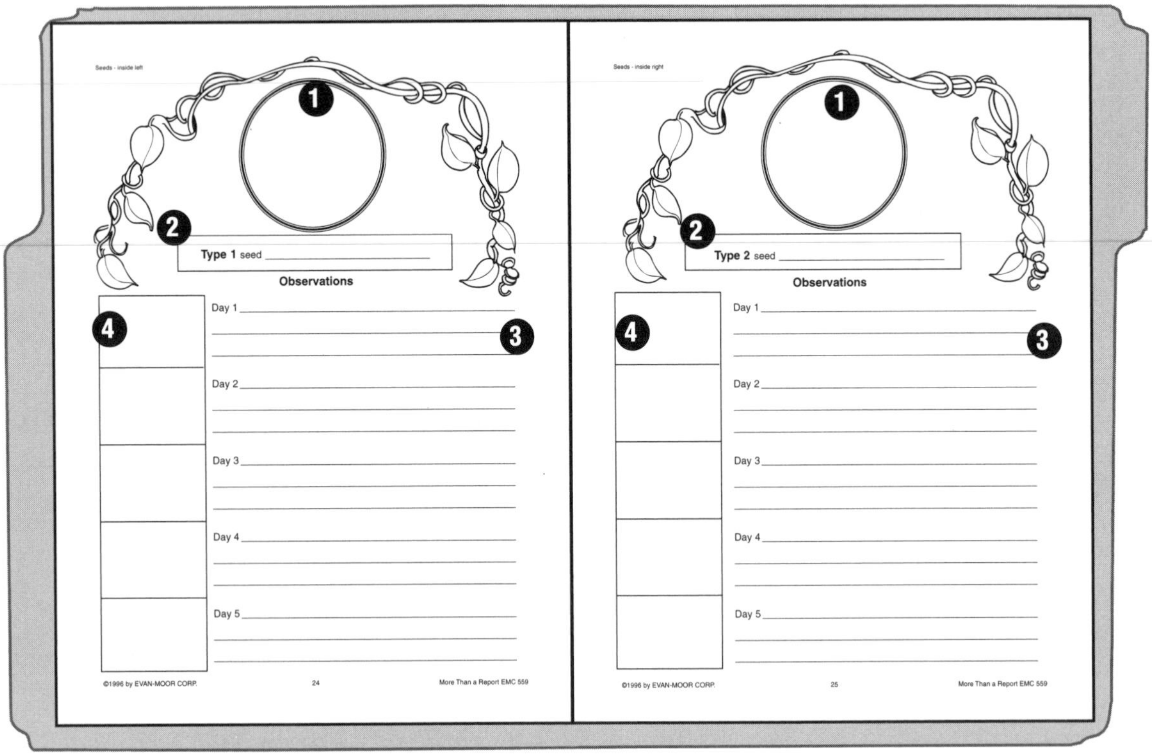

Instructions—The diagram above shows the different parts of your report. The numbers in your directions match the numbers above. This shows you where information is to be placed on your report. Keep these sheets in your folder so you can look at them often. You're going to do a ***life-giving*** job!

☐ **Front Cover**

Your front cover is not pictured here. To complete the front cover, follow these directions:

- Show your seeds on the cover as a fully grown plants.
- Be accurate in your drawing.
- Color carefully.
- Fill in the information on the lines at the bottom.

Name: _____

☐ **❶ Seed Cups**

When your seed-growing period is over, your seed cups will be displayed in these circles.

- Line the cups with the cotton.

- Add water to each cup, allowing the cotton to soak up the water and remain moist.

- Place the seed the teacher gave you between the cotton and the side of one cup.

- Place the seed you brought between the cotton and the side of the other cup.

- Write your name and the seed name on each cup with a permanent marker.

- Place your cups in the area your teacher has designated.

- Add water when the cotton begins to dry out.

☐ **❷ Type of Seed**

Write on each line the type of seed in that cup.

☐ **❸ Record Observations**

Each day you will record observations of both seeds.

- Write clearly using careful words to describe what you see.

- Use the correct language for the seed parts.

- Measure growth as accurately as you can.

☐ **❹ Illustrations**

- After you have recorded your observations, draw a picture of what your seed looks like each day. The box is small, so draw carefully.

- Color what you observe.

Hints for completing a "life-giving" report:

Make careful observations.

Talk about what you see with other students.

Choose your words carefully.

Draw each picture with a lot of detail.

YOUR REPORT IS DUE: _____

Seeds

Before assigning the report:

1. Assign each student to bring a seed or two from home. These can be fruit seeds, seeds from packages, or seeds from outside.

2. Prepare these materials for each student:
    *   1 file folder or folded 12" x 18" (30.5 x 46 cm) piece of construction paper
    *   report reproducibles, pages 23, 24, and 25
    *   student direction sheets, pages 26 and 27 (fill in date due before copying)
    *   2 clear plastic cups
    *   cotton to line cups (use cotton rolls)
    *   a bean seed
    *   use of a permanent black marker

3. Determine how many days you want them to observe. If more than 5 days, run more copies of the observation form on page 29.

4. Decide on an area where seed cups can be placed during the observation period.

Assigning the report:

1. Pass out to each student:
    *   folder and student reproducibles
    *   2 cups with cotton to line
    *   a bean seed
    *   student direction sheets

2. Introduce the topic. Explain that every student will observe and record their observations about two different seeds. They should follow along on their direction sheets as you explain each section of the report. (See Directions, page 3.)

Working on the report:

*   Provide students with daily observation and recording time.

*   Set aside classroom time for discussion of observations.

*   Ask your librarian for support and classroom reference materials.

Finishing the report:

*   Glue the completed report cover to the outside of the folder.

*   Glue the completed reproducibles to the inside of the folder; one on each side.

*   If observation sheets are 2 or more pages long, glue the final observation sheet to the folder and staple the earlier observation sheets to the top.

*   Display the seed cups on the open folders.

Day _____

Day _____

Day _____

Day _____

Day _____

Day _____

Day _____

29

Desert Dwellers

There are about 20 major deserts in the world, spread out on five continents. They cover almost 15% of the earth's land area—about the size of South America. The scientific definition of a desert is a place that has very little vegetation, receives less than 25 cm (10 inches) of rain each year, and has a high rate of evaporation. Many people think that the desert has as little life as it has rainfall, but this is not true. The desert is alive with many **amazing** plants and animals.

In this **More Than a Report,** students are asked to report on one desert dweller. By studying its adaptations for survival and the amazing way it hangs on to life, students will have an appreciation for all living things. They will learn to view deserts not as being "deserted," but as being abundantly full.

Complete teacher directions for **Desert Dwellers** are on page 36.

A Desert Dweller

An Amazing Report about the

_____

Prepared by: _____

On: _____ From Room: _____

glue here

Do you know the answers to the following questions

about the amazing_____?

1. _____

2. _____

3. _____

4. _____

5. _____

Keep reading to find the answers.

Deserts of the World

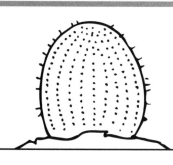

Bibliography

_____

_____

_____

_____

_____

_____

       More Than a Report EMC 559

Name: _____

The *amazing* desert dweller you are reporting on: _____

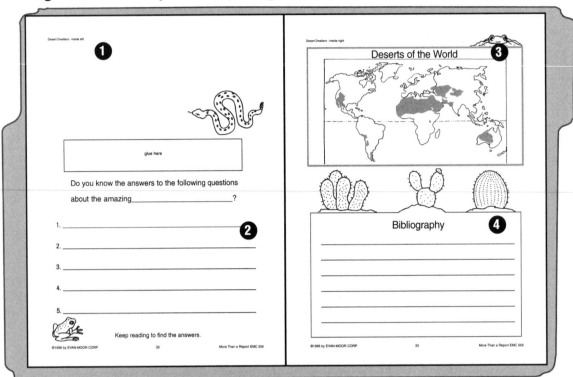

Instructions—The diagram above shows the different parts of your report. The numbers in your directions match the numbers above. This shows you where information is to be placed on your report. Keep these sheets in your folder so you can look at them often. You're going to do an *amazing* job!

☐ **Front Cover**
Your front cover is not pictured here. To complete the front cover, follow these directions:

- Fill in the line with the name of your desert dweller.
- Draw your desert dweller in the space provided.
- Fill in the information on the lines at the bottom.
- Color the illustrations.

☐ ❶ **Stand-Up Picture**
Draw a picture of your desert dweller on the folded piece of file folder your teacher has given you.

- Keep the fold at the top.
- Make the picture large, touching the top and bottom. Color it.
- Cut out the picture. Cut both layers. Leave a border.
- Glue the front lip inside the box. Do not glue the back lip.

Name: _____

☐ ❷ **Ask Five Questions**
  • Do research on your desert dweller.
  • Write the titles of books you used in the bibliography on the right inside page.
  • When you find an interesting fact, write it down.
  • Write a question that can be answered using your information.
  • Write one question on each line.
  • Make your questions interesting and different.

☐ ❸ **Deserts of the World Map**
  This map of the world shows all the major desert areas.
  • Label as many desert areas as you can.
  • Color the area(s) where your desert dweller can be found.

☐ ❹ **Mini-Book of Answers**
  This is where you will answer the questions you asked. Write the answers on the paper provided, using the lined-paper masters for neatness.
  • Page 1 - Cover - *"Amazing answers to the questions can be found here!"*
  • Use one page to answer each question; six pages in all.
  • Put a small picture on each page.
  • Your teacher will staple these in later.

Hints for completing a truly "amazing" report:

Be neat. Use your best handwriting.

Ask interesting questions and provide complete answers

Sketch your drawing lightly until you are happy with it; then trace over it darker.

Use your imagination and creativity.

YOUR REPORT IS DUE: _____

Desert Dwellers

Before assigning the report:

1. Your students will need to be able to do simple note-taking before attempting this report. If you feel they lack sufficient experience, pick a desert dweller from the list on page 37. Do the research and note taking as a group, with you modeling correct strategies.

2. Prepare the materials needed for each student:
    *   1 file folder or folded 12" x 18" (30.5 x 46 cm) piece of construction paper
    *   report reproducibles, pages 31, 32, 33
    *   student direction sheets, pages 34 and 35 (fill in date due before copying)
    *   cut file folder (see page 4)
    *   file folder cut 4" x 5" (10 x 13 cm)
    *   lined-paper masters (see directions, page 3)

3. Decide how to assign each desert dweller. (See directions, page 3, and the list of desert dwellers on page 37.)

Assigning the report:

1. Pass out to each student:
    *   folder and report reproducibles
    *   cut file folder
    *   6 cut sheets of plain paper
    *   student direction sheets
    *   index cards or note-taking paper

2. Introduce the topic. Explain that every student will report on a different desert dweller. They should follow along on their direction sheets as you explain each section of the report. (See directions, page 3.)

3. Demonstrate how their stand-up picture will look after it is cut out.

Working on the report:

*   Provide students with a variety of resources.

*   Ask your librarian for support and classroom reference materials.

*   Provide lined-paper masters.

Finishing the report:

*   Help students proofread work before it is transferred to the final copies.

*   Staple pages of answers to right-inside page.

*   Glue the completed report cover to the outside of the folder.

*   Glue the completed reproducibles to the inside of the folder; one on each side.

Desert Dwellers

Plants

saguaro cactus	elephant tree
prickly pear cactus	teddy bear cholla
barrel cactus	living stones
hedgehog cactus	pincushion cactus
ocotillo	candle plant
mesquite	fishhook barrel cactus
ghost flower	smoke tree
strawberry cactus	feather cactus
old man cactus	Joshua tree

Animals

kangaroo rats	pack rats
pocket mice	jerboas
jackrabbits	fennec foxes
gazelle	sidewinder
golden mole	gecko
roadrunner	ground squirrel
desert iguana	elf owl
kit fox	scorpion
spadefoot toad	fringe-toed lizard
turkey vulture	lubber grasshopper
coyote	ringtail
desert tortoise	peccary
mule deer	

Forests Are Not Just Trees

Forests cover nearly one-third of the continental United States. More than 700 different kinds of trees are found in U.S. forests. But **fabulous** forests are not just trees. Each forest is a complete ecosystem of plants, animals, trees, and soils. Wildlife can be found in all layers of the forest—from the canopy down to the forest floor. A single forest is comprised of many habitats: old growth forest, young forest, meadows, lakes, and rivers.

Besides sheltering wildlife, forests provide us with many products and places for recreation. Forests are also very important in protecting our soil and water supplies. They are a very complex place worthy of our study.

In this **More Than a Report**, students will report on one forest creature. Hopefully they will learn the importance of forest management as a means of protecting the valuable habitats necessary for their creature to survive.

Complete teacher directions for **Forests**... are on page 44.

Forests Are Not Just Trees

They are the home
for the fabulous

_____

This fabulous report prepared by

_____

Date _____Room _____

Forest Creature's Name:

What it looks like: _____

Where it lives: _____

What it eats: _____

About its young: _____

What makes it special: _____

_____

_____

Bibliography

_____

_____

_____

_____

_____

_____

_____

Protect Our Forests

Name:_____

The *fabulous* forest creature you are reporting on:_____

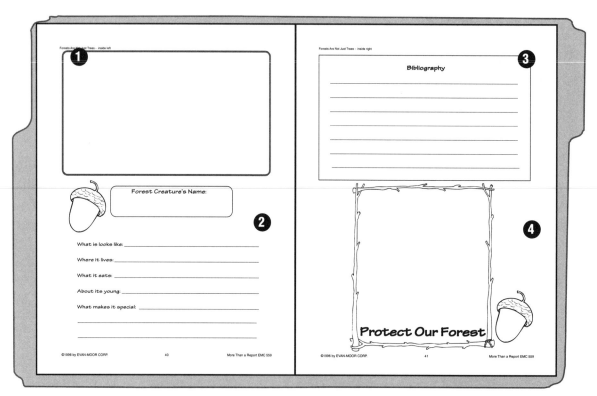

Instructions—The diagram above shows the different parts of your report. The numbers in your directions match the numbers above. This shows you where information is to be placed on your report. Keep these sheets in your folder so you can look at them often. You're going to do a *fabulous* job!

☐ **Front Cover**
Your front cover is not pictured here. To complete the front cover, follow these directions:

- Write the name of your forest creature on the line.

- Draw an color a picture of the animal. Add background as well.

- Fill in the information at the bottom.

☐ **❶ Cardboard Forest**
Using the cardboard piece and small file folder pieces, you will construct a forest.

- Using the tip of a pair of scissors, cut 6 narrow 1" (2.5 cm) slits in the top layer of your piece of cardboard.

- Cut the file folder pieces as shown, making one-inch-wide tabs that will fit into the slits in the cardboard.

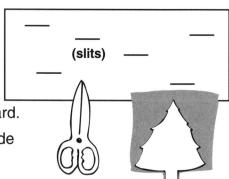

Name: _____

- Of the six pieces:

  1 is to be a picture of your creature

  3 are to be trees

  2 are to be shrubs or bushes

- Draw them large and detailed. Color and cut, being careful not to cut off the tab.

- Spread a layer of white glue on the cardboard; sprinkle with dirt and small leaves; let dry.

- Glue picture tabs in the slits.

☐ **❷ Creature Information**

  - Fill in the information neatly and accurately.

☐ **❸ Mini-Book**

This is a space for a six-page mini-book. Choose 5 of the words listed below. Put one word on each page and write a paragraph that describes what it is and how it relates to forests. Write your final copy using the lined masters your teacher has provided.

- *page 1:*   cover - ***Forests Are Fabulous Places***
- *pages 2-6:*

forests	meadows
deforestation	conifer
habitat	deciduous trees
diversity	forest management

☐ **❹ Poster**

In this place, design a poster.

- Give at least 2 reasons why forests should be protected.

- Draw pictures to support your reasons.

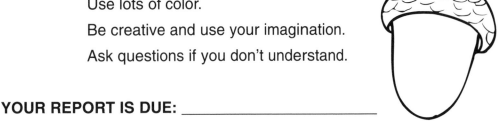

Hints for completing a truly "fabulous" report:

Be neat. Use your best handwriting.

Use lots of color.

Be creative and use your imagination.

Ask questions if you don't understand.

YOUR REPORT IS DUE: _____

Forests Are Not Just Trees

TEACHER DIRECTIONS

Before assigning the report:
1. Your students will need to be able to do simple note-taking before attempting this report. If you feel they lack sufficient experience, pick a forest creature and do the research and note taking as a group with you modeling correct strategies.

2. Prepare the materials needed for each student:
   - 1 file folder or folded 12" x 18" (30.5 x 46 cm) piece of construction paper
   - report reproducibles, pages 39, 40, and 41
   - student direction sheets, pages 42 and 43 (fill in date due before copying)
   - one- 7" x 4" (18 x 10 cm) piece of cardboard
   - 6 file-folder pieces cut to various sizes for trees, shrubs, and creatures
   - 6 sheets of plain paper, cut 7" x 4" (18 x 10 cm), for answering questions
   - dirt and small leaves
   - glue
   - lined-paper masters (see directions, page 3)

3. Decide how to assign each forest creature (see directions, page 3, and the list of forest creatures on page 45).

Assigning the report:
1. Pass out to each student:
   - folder and report reproducibles
   - various sizes of cut file folders
   - 6 sheets of plain paper
   - student direction sheets

2. Introduce the topic. Explain that every student will report on a different forest creature. They should follow along on their direction sheets as you explain each section of the report (see directions, page 3 and the list of possible topics on page 45).

Working on the report:
- Provide students with a variety of resources.
- Ask your librarian for support and classroom reference materials.
- Set aside a newspaper-covered area to glue the dirt and small leaves to the cardboard.
- Provide lined-paper masters.

Finishing the report:
- Help students proofread work before it is transferred to the final copies.
- Staple pages of mini-book to right-inside page.
- Glue the completed report cover to the outside of the folder.
- Glue the completed reproducibles to the inside of the folder; one on each side.

FOREST CREATURES

red-backed salamander

porcupine

wood stork

ruffed grouse

earthworm

deer mouse

white-tailed deer

black-capped chickadee

black bear

beaver

barred owl

box turtle

rainbow trout

chipmunk

wood duck

caribou

American toad

copperhead

golden mouse

banana slug

northern spotted owl

ground beetle

eastern gray squirrel

red fox

pleated woodpecker

wild turkey

common loon

river otter

garter snake

largemouth bass

beaver

elk

moose

gray fox

mountain lion

skunk

Minerals

A mineral is a solid, homogenous, crystalline chemical element or compound that results from inorganic processes.

All rocks found in the earth's crust are made up of minerals such as those you see in jewelry cases or at museums. Even though the rocks you see may not be as **beautiful** as the showcase models, they are still composed of the same matter. There are between 1,300 and 1,400 different minerals in the earth's crust.

A mineral in its natural shape is called a crystal. In igneous rocks, the crystals are sometimes well formed. Sedimentary rocks do not usually show good crystal shapes.

In this **More Than a Report,** students will examine a particular mineral, look at its properties and examine its uses.

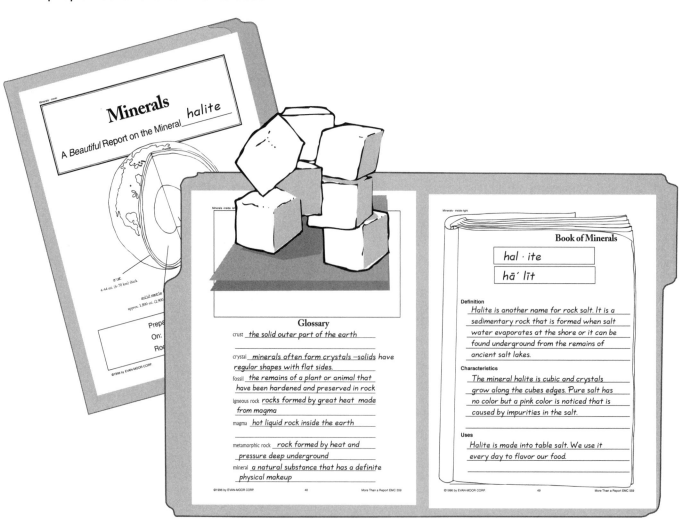

Complete teacher directions for **Minerals** are on page 52.

Minerals

A *Beautiful* Report on the Mineral_____

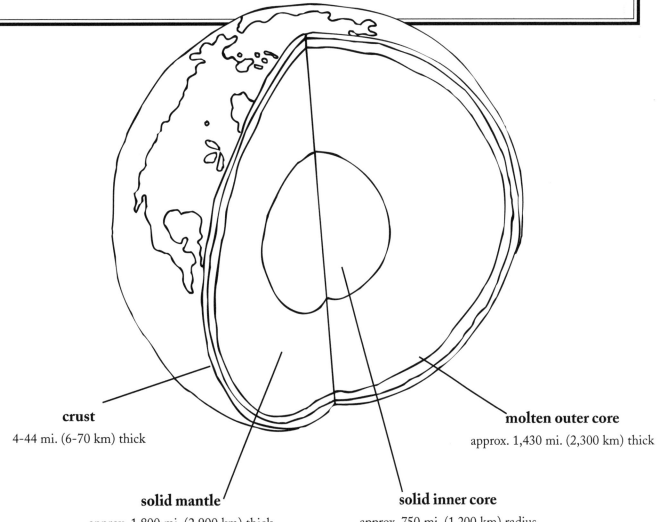

crust
4-44 mi. (6-70 km) thick

molten outer core
approx. 1,430 mi. (2,300 km) thick

solid mantle
approx. 1,800 mi. (2,900 km) thick

solid inner core
approx. 750 mi. (1,200 km) radius

Prepared by: _____

On: _____

Room: _____

       More Than a Report EMC 559

Glossary

crust _____

_____

crystal _____

_____

fossil _____

_____

igneous rock _____

_____

magma _____

_____

metamorphic rock _____

_____

mineral _____

_____

Book of Minerals

Definition

_____

_____

_____

_____

_____

Characteristics

_____

_____

_____

_____

_____

Uses

_____

_____

_____

Name: _____

The **beautiful mineral** you are reporting on: _____

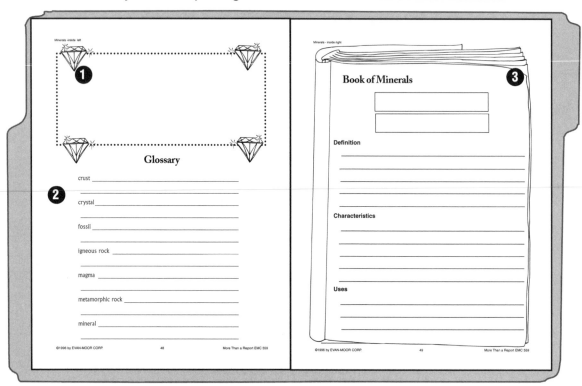

Instructions—The diagram above shows the different parts of your report. The numbers in your directions match the numbers above. This shows you where information is to be placed on your report. Keep these sheets in your folder so you can look at them often. You're going to do a **beautiful** job!

☐ **Front Cover**
Your front cover is not pictured here. To complete the front cover, follow these directions:
• Fill in the top line with the name of your mineral.

• Color the picture of the earth.

• Fill in the information at the bottom.

☐ ❶ **Decorated Rock**
Use the rock you chose or your teacher gave you and decorate it to resemble your mineral. It will be on display in this space.
• Do your research first.

• You can use paint, crayons, aluminum foil, plastic wrap, or other supplies that are available.

• You may also add extra features (crushed macaroni, smaller rocks, etc.) to achieve a certain shape and texture.

• Secure the rock to the cardboard when it is finished. White glue works, but needs to dry overnight without being touched. A glue gun works well but needs to be used by an adult.

Name: _____

☐ ❷ **Glossary**
Part of your report includes a glossary.

- Write definitions for each word.

- Write them in your own words.

- Make sure they are complete and accurate.

- Write neatly.

☐ ❸ **Reference Book Entry**
You are going to write your own reference book entry for your mineral.

- Top box - Print the mineral's name, dividing between syllables.

- Box 2 - Write the word to show its pronunciation. Include pronunciation symbols.

- Definition - Write a clear, concise definition in your own words. State the type of rock it can be found in (for example, igneous...).

- Characteristics - List its various colors, luster, hardness, and other distinguishing features.

- Uses - List its various uses in the everyday world.

- Include small illustrations if space permits.

Hints for completing a truly "beautiful" report:

Be neat. Use your best handwriting.

Do careful and thorough research using many sources.

Plan carefully how to transform your rock into your mineral.

Be creative and use your imagination.

Ask questions if you don't understand something.

YOUR REPORT IS DUE: _____

Before assigning the report:

1. Your students will need to be able to do simple note taking before attempting this report. If you feel they lack sufficient experience, pick a mineral from the list on page 53. Do the research and note taking as a group, with you modeling correct strategies.

2. Prepare the materials needed for each student:
   • 1 file folder or folded 12" x 18" (30.5 x 46 cm) piece of construction paper
   • report reproducibles, pages 47, 48, and 49
   • student directions sheets, pages 50 and 51
   • 1 piece of cardboard, cut 7" x 4" (18 x 10 cm)
   • 1 rock, approximately fist size, varying shapes

3. Decide how to assign each mineral (see directions, page 3 and the list of minerals on page 53).

4. A glue gun will be very helpful in gluing the rock to the cardboard.

Assigning the report:

1. Pass out to each student:
   • folder and report reproducibles
   • cardboard
   • rock
   • note-taking paper

2. Introduce the topic. Explain that every student will report on a different mineral. They should follow along on their direction sheets as you explain each section of the report.

Working on the report:

• Provide students with a variety of resources.

• Ask your librarian for support and classroom reference materials.

• Set aside classroom time to work on reports and provide materials to work on rocks.

• Set aside a spot to decorate rocks.

Finishing the report:

• Glue the completed report cover to the outside of the folder.

• Glue the completed reproducibles to the inside of the folder; one on each side.

• Glue the decorated rock to the piece of cardboard with white glue or a hot glue gun.

Note: You may wish to photocopy each student's mineral reference-book entry and create a class reference book on minerals.

agate	halite
amethyst	hematite
apatite	jasper
bauxite	malachite
beryl	mica
calcite	opal
carnelian	peridot
cinnabar	platinum
copper	pyrite
corundum	quartz
diamond	silver
dolomite	soapstone
feldspar	sulphur
fluorite	talc
garnet	topaz
gold	tourmaline
gypsum	turquoise

Life in the Ocean

With over 70% of our planet covered with water, it is important that students develop an understanding of this liquid environment and the creatures who live there. Even if they live far from the coast, students will be fascinated to learn about strange creatures that never see light or underwater mountains taller than Mount Everest.

Use this **fascinating *More Than a Report*** in conjunction with a visit to an aquarium or as a component of a science unit. As students learn about the treasures of the ocean, they will be more likely to work to protect this vital environment.

Complete teacher direction for *Life in the Ocean* are on page 60.

Life in the Ocean

A Fascinating Day

in the Life of

_____

Researched and illustrated by: _____

Date _____   Room _____

Glue the bottom half of the pop-up page here.

Facts about the *fascinating* _____

Size: _____

Color:_____

Identifying characteristics:_____

_____

Where it can be found: _____

Bibliography

_____

_____

_____

_____

_____

_____

_____

Word Web

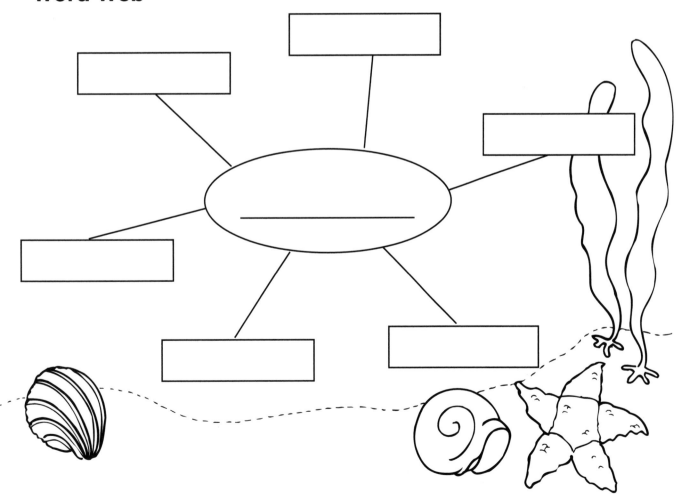

The fascinating sea creature you are reporting on is: _____

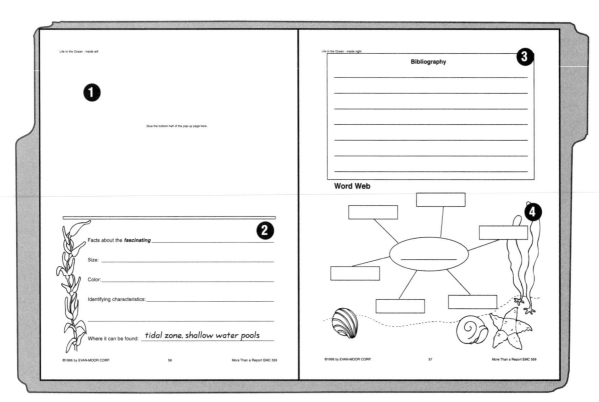

Instructions—The diagram above shows the different parts of your report. The numbers in your directions match the numbers above. This shows you where information is to be placed on your report. Keep these sheets in your folder so you can look at them often. You're going to do a *fascinating* job!

☐ **Front Cover**
Your front cover is not pictured here. To complete the front cover, follow these directions:

- Fill in the line with the name of your sea creature.

- Draw a picture of it.

- Fill in the information at the bottom.

☐ **❶ Pop-Up Page**
Follow your teacher's directions for folding and cutting the pop-up form.

- Color the ocean.

- Draw your ocean creature. Color and cut it out. Glue it to any any pop-up tab.

- Draw, color, and cut other sea plants and animals that you would find in this environment. Glue them on the other pop-up tabs.

- Follow your teacher's directions for gluing the pop-up to a construction paper folder.

Name: _____

☐ ❷ **Facts**
Fill in information accurately. You do not need to write in complete sentences.

☐ ❸ **Mini-Book**
This is a space for a six-page mini-book. Do your research first, taking notes.
Record the books you use in the bibliography space located on the inside right page.
Write your final copy using the lined masters your teacher provides. This report will
be written as if you are the sea creature. Answering the questions below will help
you start. Begin each page like this:

- *page 1* - Title page: **"A FASCINATING Day in the Life of _____"**

- *page 2* - **Moving around is fun.**
    Is it slow or fast? How do you move? Why do you move?

- *page 3* - **It's time to eat.**
    What do you eat? How do you eat?

- *page 4* - **Reproducing is part of my life.**
    How are your young born? How many? Where?

- *page 5* - **Hiding from my enemies is important.**
    How do you hide? Who do you hide from?

- *page 6* - **Help protect my environment.**
    How can people help protect the ocean?

☐ ❹ **Word Web**

- Write your creature's name in the circle.

- Write one good descriptive word or scientific fact in each box.

Hints for completing a truly "fascinating" report:

Be neat. Use your best handwriting.

Use lots of color.

Use many different resources for your report.

Be creative and use your imagination.

YOUR REPORT IS DUE: _____

Life in the Ocean

Before assigning the report:
1. Your students will need to be able to do simple note taking before attempting this report. If you feel they lack sufficient experience, pick an ocean creature from page 62 and do the research and note taking as a group, with you modeling correct strategies.

2. Prepare the materials needed for each student:
    - 1 file folder or folded 12" x 18" (30.5 x 46 cm) piece of construction paper
    - report reproducibles, pages 55, 56, and 57
    - pop-up form, page 61
    - student direction sheets, pages 58 and 59 (fill in date due before copying)
    - 1 piece colored construction paper, 8 1/2" x 11" (21.5 x 28 cm), for pop-up backing
    - paper for drawing sea creatures for pop-up page
    - 6 sheets of plain paper, cut 7" x 4" (18 x 10 cm), for mini-book

3. Decide how to assign each sea creature (see directions, page 3, and the list of ocean creatures on page 62).

Assigning the report:
1. Pass out to each student:
    - folder and report reproducibles
    - construction paper
    - 6 cut sheets of plain paper
    - student direction sheets
    - index cards or note-taking paper

2. Introduce the topic. Explain that every student will report on a different sea creature. They should follow along on their direction sheets as you explain each section of the report.

3. Directions for the pop-up page are on page 5. After students have had time to research their animal, you may wish to do the pop-up page together.

4. Model how to write the mini-book in "first person."

Working on the report:
- Provide students with a variety of resources.
- Ask your librarian for support and classroom reference materials.
- Set aside classroom time to work on reports and materials to work on pop-up page.
- Provide lined-paper masters (see directions, page 3).

Finishing the report:
- Help students proofread work before it is transferred to the final copies.
- Glue the completed report cover to the outside of the folder.
- Staple pages of the mini-book onto the right-inside page.
- Glue the completed reproducibles to the inside of the folder; one on each side.
- Glue down the bottom of the completed pop-up page.

cut

cut

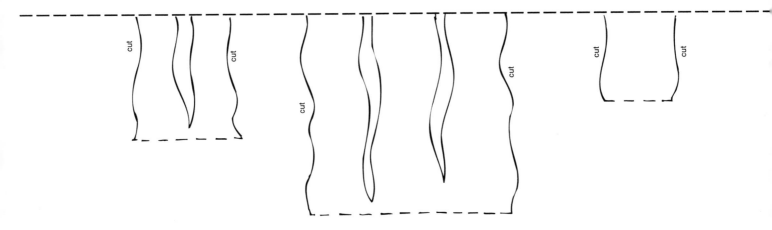

cut

cut

cut

cut

cut

cut

cut

cut

cut

cut

Life in the Ocean

Tidal Zone:

barnacle	sea urchin
limpet	star fish
mussel	brittle sea star
sand dollar	sea anemone
clam	hermit crab
fiddler crab	scallop
lugworm	sea horse

Sunlight Zone:

Portuguese man-of-war	flying fish
sea turtles	rattail fish
sunfish	octopus
dolphin	swordfish
sperm whale	manta ray
blue marlin	flying fish
bluefin tuna	herring
thresher shark	albacore

Twilight Zone:

lantern fish	black devil
viperfish	tripod fishlantern fish
hatchet fish	angler fish
mid-water jellyfish	squid
opossum shrimp	black swallower
snipe eel	

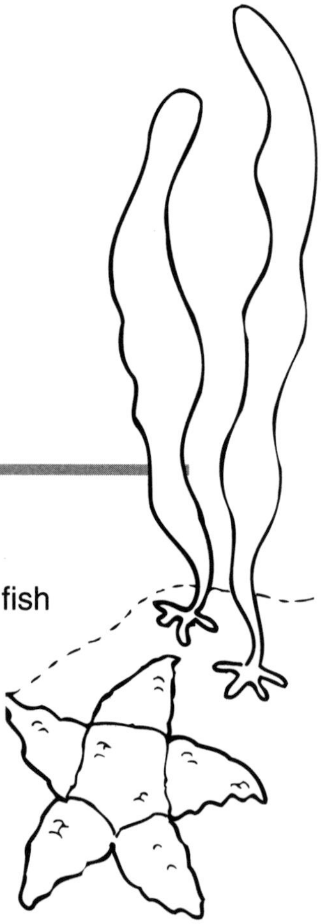

Save the Earth

Nobody made a greater mistake
than he who did nothing
because he could only do a little.
-Edmund Burke

When the population of the earth was smaller, and industrialization was restricted to a few western nations, it was possible to ignore the effects of modern life on the ecology of our planet.

No longer—the holes in the ozone are increasing; our oxygen-creating rainforests are decreasing, and deserts are expanding world-wide.

The children you teach today will inherit a very different Earth tomorrow if we fail to act now.

This **vital *More Than a Report*** makes an excellent culmination to an ecology or Earth Day unit.

Complete teacher directions for **Save the Earth** are on page 70.

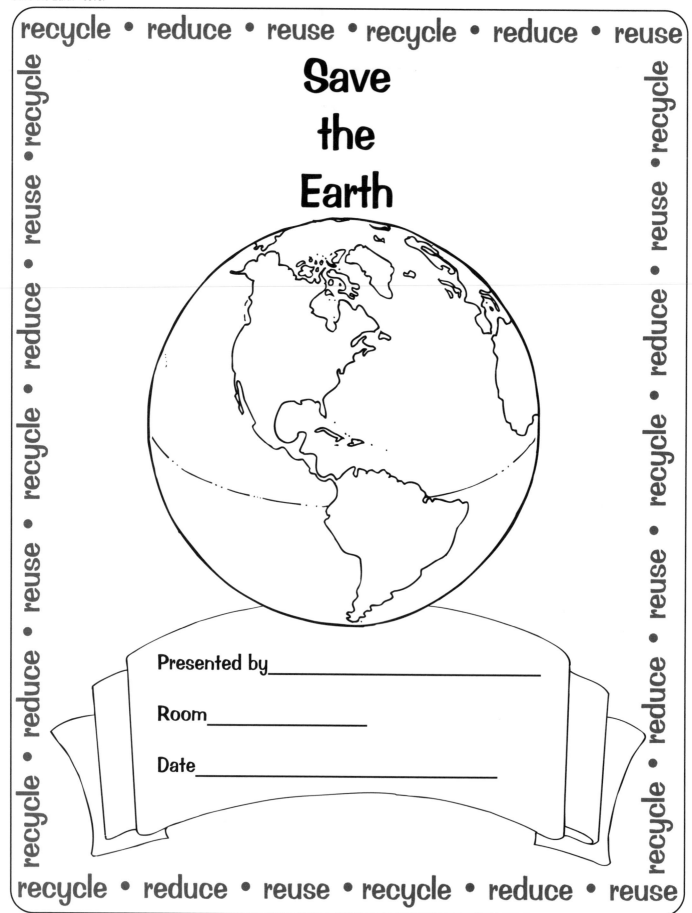

Save
the
Earth

Presented by_____

Room_____

Date_____

recycle • reduce • reuse • recycle • reduce • reuse

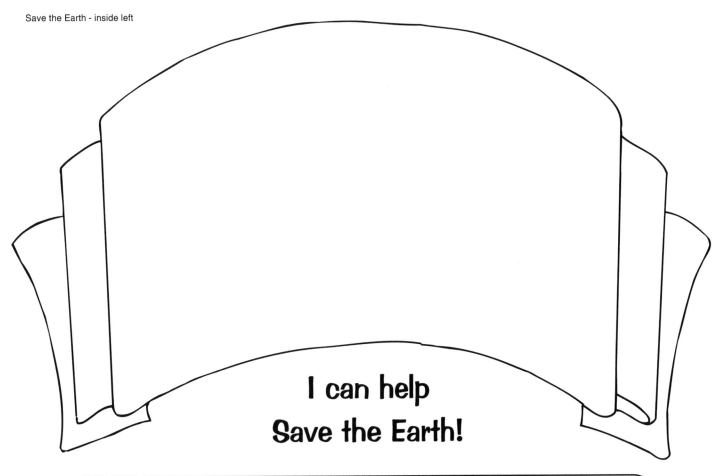

I can help
Save the Earth!

Four ways I can do this:

1. _____

_____

2. _____

_____

3. _____

_____

4. _____

_____

Glue pop-up here.

reduce

reuse

Glue pop-up here.

Glue pop-up here.

recycle

Glue pop-up here.

Name: _____

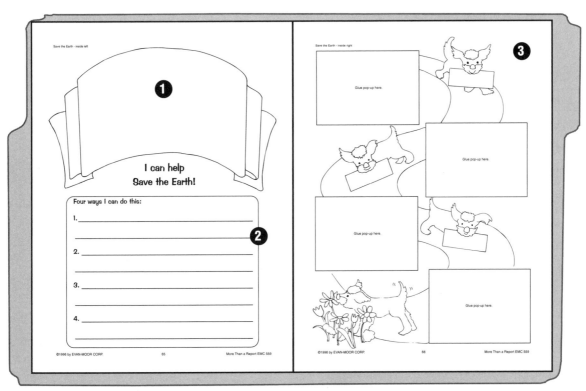

Instructions—The diagram above shows the different parts of your report. The numbers in your directions match the numbers above. This shows you where information is to be placed on your report. Keep these sheets in your folder so you can look at them often. You're going to do a *vital* job!

☐ **Front Cover**
Your front cover is not pictured here. To complete the front cover, follow these directions:

- Color the earth.

- Fill in the information at the bottom.

☐ ❶ **Banner**
Create your own imaginative, colorful banner that will convince people of the need to reduce, reuse, recycle.

☐ ❷ **Four Ways to Save the Earth**
- List 4 ways that you will help save the earth.

- Write clearly and simply.

- Make each way different.

- Remember the three R's: , **reduce**, **reuse**, **recycle**

Name:_____

□ ❸ **Pop-Up Page**

- Follow the directions your teacher gives for folding and cutting the four pop-ups. *(pictures 1-3)*

- On each small piece of drawing paper, draw and color an item which represents a way you will help save the earth. Refer to what you wrote on the banner.

- Cut out each item and glue it to one of the pop-up tabs. *(pictures 4 and 5)*

- Color and cut out the pop-up covers.

- Follow your teacher's directions for gluing the pop-ups into the covers. *(picture 6)*

- After the pages of your report are glued into the folder, you will glue the back of each pop-up cover to a space on the report form.

1.

4.

2.

5.

3.

6.

Glue backsides of each half of the pop-up to the inside of the cover.

Hints for completing a truly "vital" report:

Be neat. Use your best handwriting.

Use lots of color.

Be creative and use your imagination.

Ask questions if you don't understand or get stuck.

YOUR REPORT IS DUE: _____

Before assigning the report:
1. Prepare the materials needed for each student:
   - •1 file folder or folded 12" x 18" (30.5 x 46 cm) piece of construction paper
   - • report reproducibles, pages 64, 65, and 66
   - • pop-up forms and covers, pages 70 and 71
   - • student direction sheets, pages 67 and 68 (fill in date due before copying)
   - • paper to draw items for the pop-up pages
2. Conduct a class discussion about "Earth-saving practices." List as many ideas as the class can come up with.

Assigning the report:
1. Pass out to each student:
   - • folder and report reproducibles
   - • student direction sheets
2. Introduce the topic. Explain that every student will report four ways they can help save the earth. They should follow along on their direction sheets as you explain each section of the report.
3. Directions for creating the pop-ups are on page 5 and in the student's directions. After students have completed page 65, you may wish to do the pop-ups together.

Working on the report:
- • Provide students with a variety of resources.
- • Ask your librarian for support and reference materials.
- • Set aside classroom time to work on pop-up projects.

Finishing the report:
- • Help students proofread work before it is transferred to the final copies.
- • Glue the completed report cover to the outside of the folder.
- • Glue the completed reproducibles to the inside of the folder; one on each side.
- • Glue the completed pop-ups to the inside-right page.

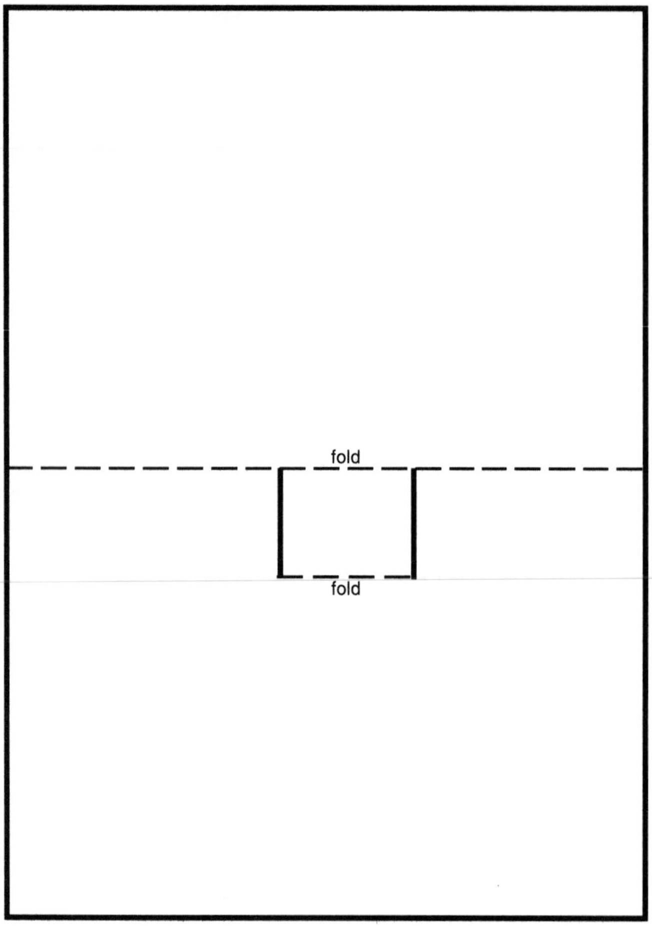

fold

fold

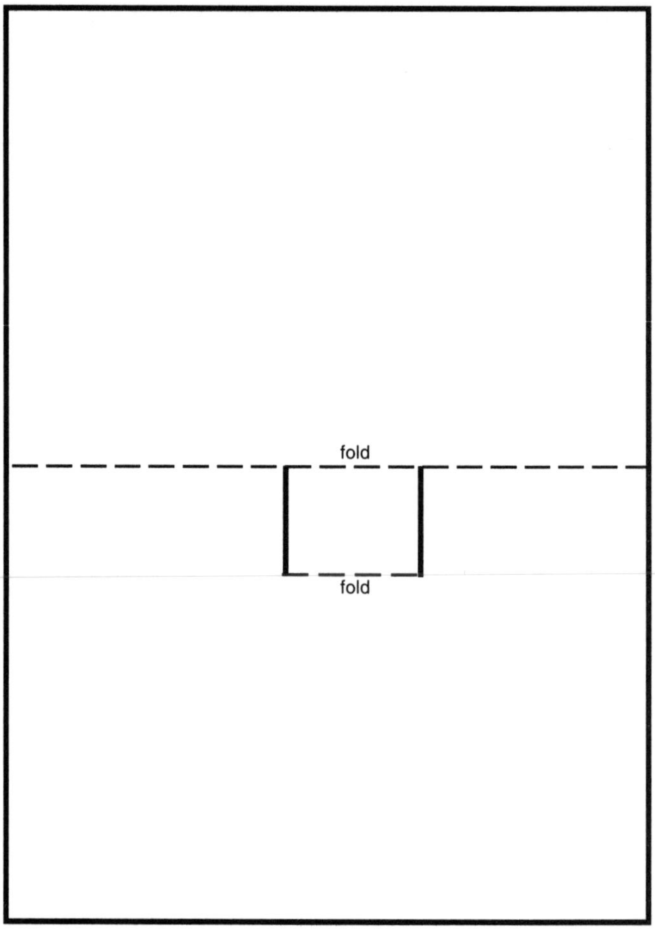

fold

fold

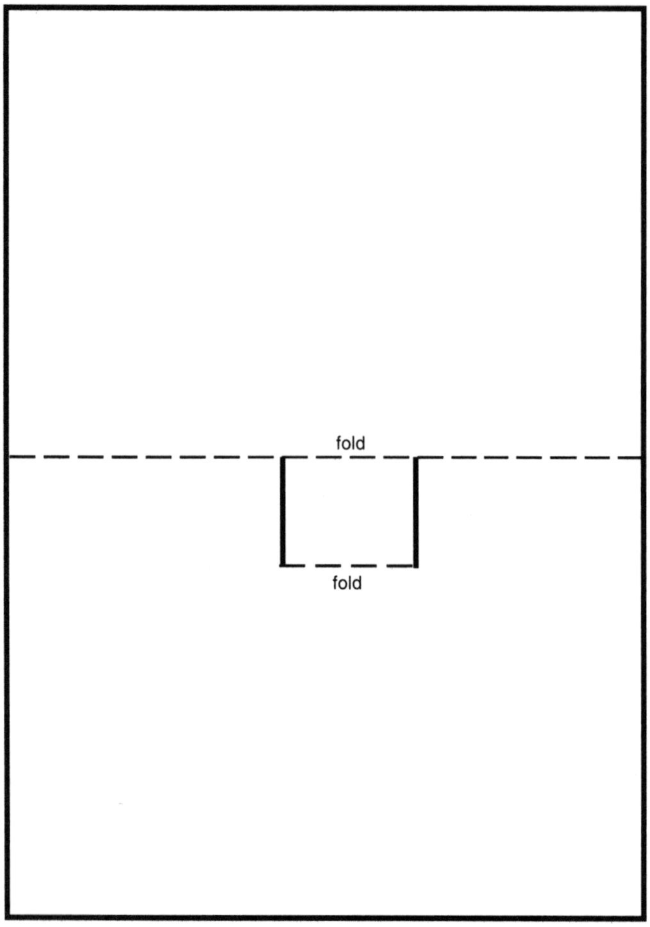

fold

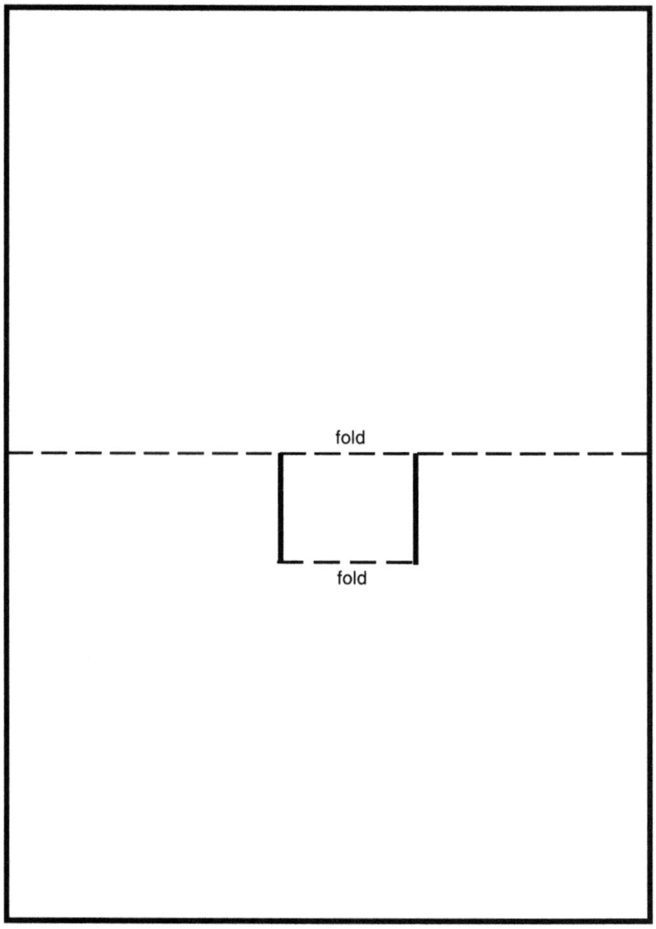

fold

fold

fold

 More Than a Report EMC 559

Endangered Animals

Before people walked the earth, only one out of a million species died of natural causes every year. How do our records compare? With pesticides, pollutants, and chainsaws, we are killing tens of thousands of the thirty-three million known species every year. Despite major conservation efforts, ecologists estimate that within thirty years we will have lost at least one-fifth of the planet's life-forms forever. Pretty scary, huh?

Endangered animals need our help. Through the education of our students, we can help to change attitudes that are selfish and destructive toward nature to attitudes that are generous and sensitive.

In this **More Than a Report**, students will report on one **important** endangered animal and learn what we can all do to aid in its survival.

Complete teacher directions for **Endangered Animals** are on page 78.

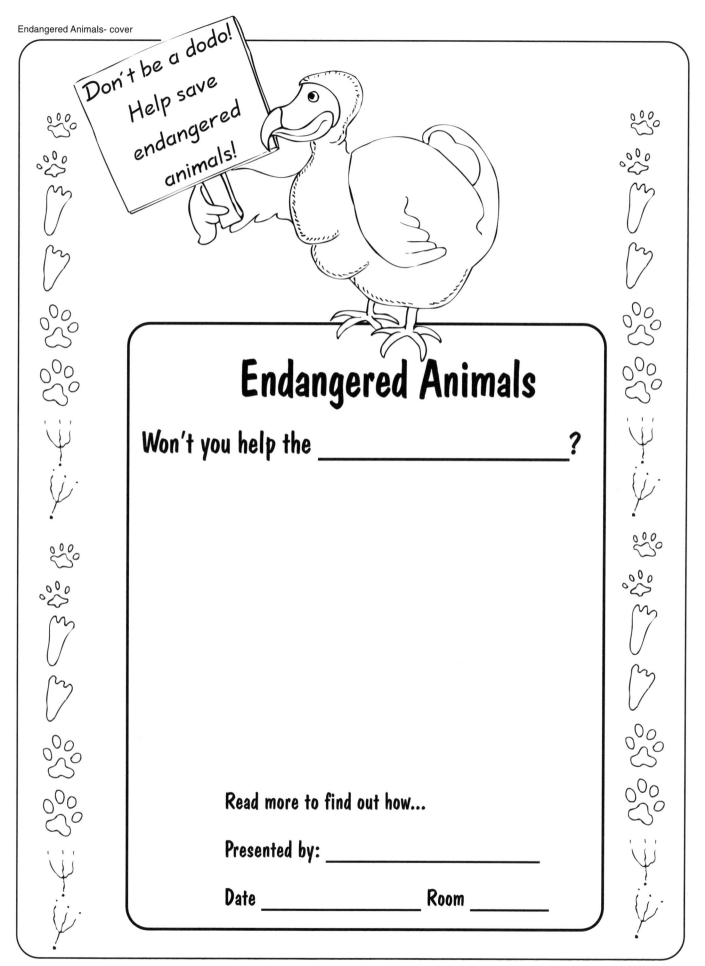

Don't be a dodo! Help save endangered animals!

Endangered Animals

Won't you help the _____?

Read more to find out how...

Presented by: _____

Date _____ Room _____

Bibliography

_____

_____

_____

_____

_____

_____

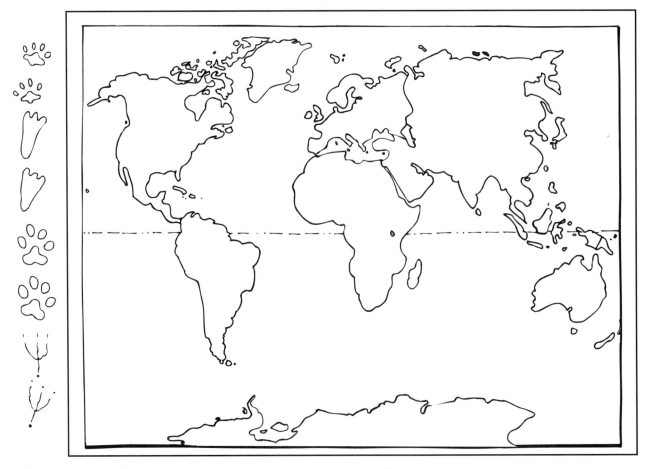

The endangered _____ *is still found in* _____ .

 More Than a Report EMC 559

Glue the bottom half of the pop-up page here.

Important Facts

Name _____

Scientific Name _____

How many are alive today? _____

Interesting facts: _____

Name: _____

The *important* endangered animal you are reporting on: _____

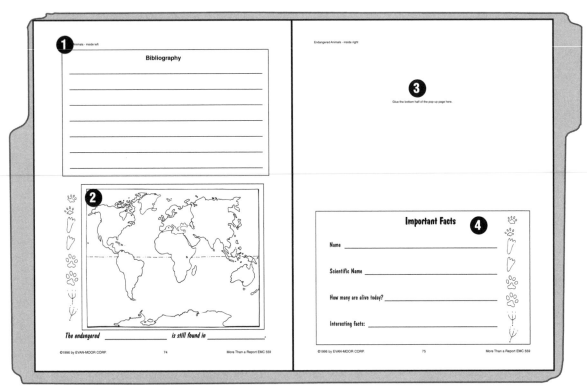

Instructions—The diagram above shows the different parts of your report. The numbers in your directions match the numbers above. This shows you where information is to be placed on your report. Keep these *important* job!

☐ **Front Cover**
Your front cover is not pictured here. To complete the front cover, follow these directions:
- Fill in the line with the name of your endangered animal.

- Draw a picture of it in the box. Color it.

- Fill in the information at the bottom.

☐ ❶ **Mini-Book**
This is a space for a six page mini-book. Do your research first, taking notes. Record the books you used in the bibliography located on your left inside page. Write your final copy using the lined masters your teacher has. This mini-book will be in the form of an interview. Answer each question as if you are that creature. When you do your final copy, write **the question** and **the answer** on the same page.

Student Directions: **Endangered Animals** *(continued)*

- *Page 1* - Title page
  "Information about the important endangered animal _____
  Read this before it is too late"
- *Page 2* - "How would you describe your appearance?"
- *Page 3* - "What sort of habitat surrounds you and why do you live there?"
- *Page 4* - "How do you protect yourself from enemies?"
- *Page 5* - "Why are you on the endangered animals list?"
- *Page 6* - "What can people do to help?

❷ **World Map**
Carefully shade in the areas where your endangered animal now lives.

❸ **Pop-Up Page**

- Follow the directions your teacher gives for folding and cutting the pop-up form.
- Draw and color the background so that it is appropriate for your creature (ocean, jungle, swamp, meadow, etc.).
- Draw your endangered animal on a plain sheet of paper. Color and cut it out. Glue it to any pop-up surface of your page. Be sure it closes correctly before gluing.
- Draw, color, and cut other plants and animals that you would find in this environment. Glue them on also.

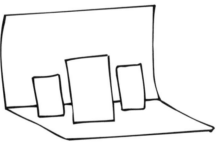

❹ **Facts**
Fill in information accurately and completely.

Hints for completing a truly "important" report:

Be neat. Use your best handwriting.

Use lots of color.

Use many different resources for your report.

Be creative and use your imagination.

YOUR REPORT IS DUE: _____

Endangered Animals

Before assigning the report:

1. Your students will need to be able to do simple note-taking before attempting this report. If you feel they lack sufficient experience, pick a topic from the list on page 80. Do the research and note taking as a group, with you modeling the correct strategies.

2. Prepare the materials needed for each student:
   - 1 file folder or folded 12" x 18" (30.5 x 46 cm) piece of construction paper
   - report reproducibles, pages 73, 74, and 75
   - pop-up page, page 79
   - student direction sheets, pages 76 and 77 (fill in date due before copying)
   - 1 piece colored construction paper, 8 1/2" x 11" (21.5 x 28 cm), for pop-up backing
   - paper for drawing endangered species for pop-up page
   - 6 sheets of plain paper, cut 7" x 4" (18 x 10 cm), for mini-book

3. Decide how to assign each animal (see directions, page 3, and list of animals on page 80).

Assigning the report:

1. Pass out to each student:
   - folder and report reproducibles
   - cut construction paper
   - 6 cut sheets of plain paper
   - student direction sheets
   - index cards or note-taking paper

2. Introduce the topic. Explain that every student will report on a different endangered animal. They will follow along on their direction sheets as you explain each section.

3. Directions for the pop-up form appear on page 5. After students have had time to research their animal, you may wish to do the pop-up together.

Working on the report:
- Provide students with a variety of resources.
- Ask your librarian for support and classroom reference materials.
- Set aside classroom time to work on reports and materials to work on pop-up page.
- Provide lined-paper masters (see directions, page 3).

Finishing the report:
- Help students proofread work before it is transferred to the final copies.
- Staple pages of the mini-book onto left-inside page.
- Glue the completed report cover to the outside of the folder.
- Glue the completed reproducibles to the inside of the folder; one on each side.
- Glue down the bottom of the completed pop-up page onto the right-inside page.

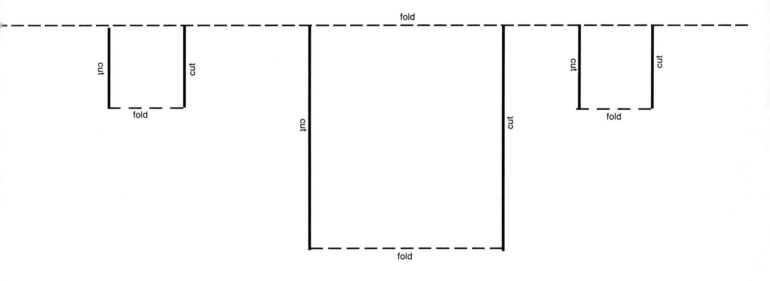

Endangered Animals

American alligator	key deer
American buffalo	lemur
black-footed ferret	margay
caiman	Mexican grizzly bear
California condor	mountain lion
capybara	nene
cougar	peccary
eastern brown pelican	puma
echidna	quetzal
emu	red wolf
fennec	swift fox
hartebeest	tapir
Hawaiian monk seal	vicuna
ibex	wallaby
ibis	walrus
ivory-billed woodpecker	whooping crane
jerboa	wombat
	yak

Note: The animals named here were on the endangered animals list in 1995. You may wish to get a more recent list and make changes as needed.